LORD, SAVE *ALL* OF ME!

Make Me Whole: Spirit, Mind, and Body

Rev. Theresa Mangano

WestBow
PRESS
A DIVISION OF THOMAS NELSON

WestBow Press books may be ordered through booksellers or by contacting:

WestBow Press
A Division of Thomas Nelson
1663 Liberty Drive
Bloomington, IN 47403
www.westbowpress.com
1-(866) 928-1240

Because of the dynamic nature of the Internet, any web addresses or
links contained in this book may have changed since publication and
may no longer be valid. The views expressed in this work are solely those
of the author and do not necessarily reflect the views of the publisher,
and the publisher hereby disclaims any responsibility for them.

Any people depicted in stock imagery provided by Thinkstock are
models, and such images are being used for illustrative purposes only.
Certain stock imagery © Thinkstock.

All Scripture quotations are taken from the Holy Bible,
Old and New King James translation, accessed from
Biblegateway.com unless otherwise indicated.

ISBN: 978-1-4908-0264-0 (sc)
ISBN: 978-1-4908-0265-7 (e)

Library of Congress Control Number: 2013912977

Printed in the United States of America.

WestBow Press rev. date: 10/29/2013

DEDICATION:

This book is dedicated first and foremost to Jesus, my Lord and Savior, the Lover of my soul, and the One in whom I take delight daily. His stubborn love has delivered me from my own limitations!

Second, I dedicate this book to my family:

- To my husband, who has lovingly supported me through all my challenges, conflicts, and victories during the past two years, who patiently and calmly partners with me through every project that God sets before me. I thank God for his gracious steadfast love and faithfulness to his Lord and to me.
- To my two sons and daughter-in-law whose eagerness to follow Christ and fierce determination to honor Him in every aspect of their lives feeds my soul and blesses my heart daily.
- To the desire of my heart and my eyes: my four beautiful grandchildren whose love for Jesus shines and grows in depth with every passing day.

My greatest desire is to see them all as living examples of the principles in this book.

CONTENTS

PREFACE

My head was dizzy and I felt like I was suffocating. My chest burned and ached in pain. My heart raced; I could feel it pounding in my chest, and it wouldn't stop. I could hardly breathe and felt like I was going to pass out. There was a horrible oppression all around me, as if there was something pressing against every inch of my body trying to squeeze every bit of life out of me. This went on day and night for weeks.

I had hardly slept for months. My eyes burned and my head hurt constantly. I couldn't think. I could not concentrate on anything. I couldn't even formulate a coherent sentence to describe what I was feeling. I hadn't eaten normally for weeks; my stomach felt constantly nauseated. There is no other way to describe what I felt: as if my spirit was "trying to leave my body." I was frightened, very frightened.

Never before had I experienced anything like this. I could not take one more day or one more hour of this agony, so in panic and desperation, I called my family doctor who prescribed pills for anxiety over the phone.

Reluctantly, I got the prescription and took the pills, just so that I would be able to calm down and breathe normally again.

I had never been an anxious person; I had always been calm and in control. I had always enjoyed good health, so I thought. I had good relationships and rarely felt threatened. Yet, every symptom I was experiencing pointed to panic attacks! All I could think was, *"Why is this happening to me?"*

I was given an additional prescription for a heavy duty antacid to control chest pain and referrals to see an asthma-allergy specialist, and a cardiac doctor.

The asthma-allergy specialist determined that I indeed had asthma and was also allergic to candida. He prescribed an inhaler, but there were no instructions for the candida allergy.

I went home and used the inhaler for two days, but my symptoms immediately became worse. In tears, I shelved the inhaler.

I then went to the pharmacist to order the antacid. It would be $500.00 co pay, they said, but I could apply for financial assistance. *"Forget it,"* I said. *"I can't afford this; I'll find another way to deal with it."*

My symptoms continued. At best, I would get an hour or two of sleep at a time; about three to four hours on a good night, and that was after taking sleeping pills. I would I sit at the edge of my bed for hours at a time rocking my body back and forth trying to fight off the panic attacks. As I rocked, I would beg God to heal me, rebuking the devil and quoting all the Scriptures

I could think of for healing. Nights became endless and nighttime my worst enemy. I was tormented and exhausted all the time.

In desperation, I went to the emergency room. X-rays were taken, tests of every kind were taken. My heart rate was "normal," they said, and so was my oxygen level. I was not having a heart attack. *"Nothing appears abnormal,"* they said. I was kept overnight so doctors could observe my "behavior," and in the morning, they said to go home and make an appointment with a psychiatrist. I wanted to scream, *"Are you kidding!?"*

I left the hospital utterly frustrated and severely depressed. It was Sunday morning and on the way home, we drove past the church where I was on staff as Associate Pastor. The worship service was going on right at that moment and I was not a part of it. How could I be? I was not in any condition to lead people. A feeling of utterly hopelessness and helplessness came over me.

No doctor had helped me. It seemed that God was deaf to my prayers of faith. I was out of options. I could not even practice what I preached; I was a failure. What hope did I have now? One thing I knew, I couldn't live like this because it wasn't living; at best it was only survival. It was horrible and I had to find an answer.

I went home, turned on my computer and prayed, *"Dear God, I know you haven't forsaken me. I know you have an answer for me. Please help me find out what is going on in my body. I need Your help! Please show me what to do."* Feeling prompted by the Holy Spirit, I typed in the words, *"candida induced panic attacks"* in the search bar to see if there existed any such diagnosis associated with the things my body was experiencing.

And there it was! Website after website with information on every one of my symptoms! Everything was there: the dizziness, the inability to concentrate, the chest burning and pain, the sleeplessness, the feelings of suffocation, anxiety, all of it. I had hope!

After putting myself on a strict diet to start cleansing my body, I knew that the diet and prayer alone would not be enough; I would have to find something that would get rid of this bodily invader, and I knew it would not include drugs. I had tried that route and pills had made me worse than when I started, so I began to search for a homeopathic doctor. Finally, I was given the name of a homeopathic nutritionist.

Once in her office, she showed me results of my blood test on a computer screen right there on the spot. There they were: millions of white candida colonies which had invaded my entire body: starting in my colon, they had moved to my lungs, my brain, all my organs, and last, into my bloodstream. The invader had been identified and it was a parasite that *could* be destroyed! But, I would have to use natural remedies, not drugs.

That day, I began the long hard journey back to health. Like most people, I had lived all my life eating processed foods, taking antibiotics, and praying for healing whenever I got sick. These things worked for awhile. But after many years, my body could no longer tolerate the lack of nutrition it needed to fight back; my immune system had declined badly and had begun to break down. My body could no longer heal itself the way my Creator intended. I had no choice but to make radical lifestyle changes.

Slowly, I began to change my diet to include more "live" and "whole" foods like raw vegetables and fruits, seeds and herbs, the kinds of foods our bodies were designed to digest. I began to eliminate more man made foods and foods grown with pesticides, artificial hormones and other chemicals. I began a new system of exercise. I began to re-teach myself to remain calm in all situations and to deal immediately with negative emotions coming from conflict with others. I would no longer talk about my problems without talking about what God is doing in me. I learned to pay attention to the whole Bible and not just the parts I feel comfortable with. It was only at this point in my life that I began to understand what it meant to be completely healed and whole.

Two years later, I have eliminated all candida related illness simply by changing my lifestyle; and there were absolutely no drugs involved in my recovery! Beginning with the Holy Spirit's direction that day at my computer, God heard my cry and led me to the answers I had been desperately seeking.

Although there may come a time in my life when medicine may be needed, the answers I found set me free from constant dependence on drugs and pills.

(Remember that $500.00 prescription for antacid I mentioned? I get the same results by drinking a pinch or two of baking soda and water—for less than a penny a glass!)

It was not easy to make all the changes I listed above, but the results are worth it! I sleep well most of the time, I rarely have a headache, never have trouble breathing, I am calm and relaxed, I rarely get sick, I have lost the excess weight I used to have, and I can find peace and joy even when hurtful things happen to me.

My life has had a wonderful overhaul! God helped me change my thinking, my heart attitude, my speaking, and my actions, and *then* my body reaped the wonderful benefits!

Before writing this book, I sought God's direction through a forty day fast. Very clearly, He directed me to write down the things He was teaching me from His word and to publish them. On the last week of my fast, I read these words:

Hold fast [to] *the pattern of sound words which you have heard from me, in faith and love which are in Christ Jesus. That good thing which was committed to you, keep by the* [power of the] *Holy Spirit who dwells in us. 2 Timothy 1:13-14 NKJ*

I have indeed held fast to the things God has shown me and I have no desire to ever compromise the things that have restored my health.

In this book, I now share with you the hidden

treasures which God has revealed in His word for *your* health and well-being also. I have prayed for you, dear reader, that you will be encouraged and energized as you read.

INTRODUCTION

Everywhere I go, I meet people who need to be healed of something. Wherever I happen to be, I find Christians are seeking spiritual as well as medical answers to their questions about health. Most people are seeking physical healing or they express the need for emotional healing of some kind. They read books on these subjects, go to conferences, pray in faith, and flood the altars at church services desperately hoping for a miraculous breakthrough.

When the same people do not receive the answers they expected, they cope with their disappointment and frustration in a variety of ways. Some simply give up caring after a period of time, others get mad at God for not answering their prayers and still others begin to doubt the reality of God's promises. Often, they come to the conclusion that the miracles and healings they read about in the New Testament were only for that day and time. Because of this, so many people live in constant discouragement and without hope of a better life.

If I had to describe the lifestyle of most of these same people, it would be this: too busy, too tired, too worn out to attend church on a regular basis, stressed out, and chronically physically ill in some way. In fact, the great majority of Christians I meet on the east coast of the U. S. (where I live) appear to operate from day to day in "survival mode," just trying to get through each day, rather than enjoying a fulfilling life.

Sad to say, this description includes a *majority* of church going people I know, rather than a minority. I have encountered only a small handful of Christians who are living in peace, joy, and good health and who are serving regularly in their church. Many people have their autopilot set on "burn out mode," which appears to have become the norm rather than the exception in our American culture.

Why is this happening and what is is wrong with this picture of Jesus' church? What has happened to the good news of the gospel, the promise of "old things passed away and all things becoming new" (2 Corinthians 5:17)? What have we missed?

And what, if anything, are pastors and leaders doing to address this sad condition of the church? My observations lead me to speculate that many pastors and church leaders are also experiencing the same burn out as those they shepherd, as in my own story shared in the preface.

I believe God has provided an answer for all of us, not just a few special people, and it is found in understanding and welcoming the simplicity of the full gospel as it was originally preached by Jesus and his disciples.

One important point I wish to make before continuing is that in no way do I equate the concept of being healthy in spirit, mind and body with the idea of being free from every kind of suffering. When we decide to follow Christ, we will suffer in this world: "*Yes, and all who desire to live godly in Christ Jesus will suffer persecution.*" (*2 Timothy 3:12 NKJ*) People may experience suffering for a variety of reasons, one of which may be persecution for their faith. Please understand that I do not believe that *all* illness is synonymous with *all* suffering.

Whether you are a pastor, leader, church member, or seeker, my hope is that, you will find renewed hope as well as key concepts to renewing your physical well-being while reading this book, so that you are freer to pursue your own life calling. Where there has been a lack of teaching or misinformation, I hope to bring clarity.

It is necessary to make another point clear: I would never presume to make a judgment call on an illness you or any one else may be experiencing. It would be impossible for me to know everything God knows about you, however, that does not negate the fact that there is knowledge available in the Bible that has been either ignored or untapped which God provided for our health because He loves us!

Because I have encountered Christians who feel that their calling is to question anything that might be different from what they have been taught or have experienced, I feel it is important to remind readers that the Bible stands on its own when a concept is stated clearly and repeated throughout the Old and New Testaments. Nothing is being presented in this book based on one verse alone, but on a series of repeated themes throughout the Bible.

Regardless of what we were taught in the past, or what we have or have not experienced, we are ultimately accountable to God alone. We are called to embrace the promises God has given to us and to put them into practice:

> ***If anyone teaches otherwise*** *and does*
> *not consent to wholesome words,*
> ***even the words of our Lord Jesus Christ, and to***
> ***the doctrine which accords with godliness***,
> *he is proud, knowing nothing, but is obsessed*
> *with disputes and arguments over words,*
> *from which come envy, strife, reviling, evil suspicions,...*
> *1 Timothy 6:3-4 NKJ*

This verse implies that to ignore or to reject what is clearly taught by Jesus and is confirmed in the gospels and epistles is to be obsessed with arguing. We are charged to *cling* to what is clearly taught in the Scriptures, for therein lies our hope of complete salvation in spirit, mind and body.

CH 1: *Who is the Real You?*

You were created in God's image:

> **Then God said, "Let Us make man in Our image,**
> **according to Our likeness**; *let them have dominion,...*
> *over all the earth and over every creeping*
> *thing that creeps on the earth."*
> **So God created man in His own image;**
> **in the image of God He created him;**
> **male and female He created them.**
> *Genesis 1:26-27 NKJ*

> **God is spirit**...*John 4:24 NKJ*

Because you are created in God's image, you are a three part being in the same way God is. That means you were created as a spiritual being, (God is a spirit) with a soul (you have a mind and emotions just like God does), and you have a body (your spiritual dwelling or house, just like Jesus). This can be pictured by concentric circles or a pyramid:

DIAGRAM A: DIAGRAM B:

 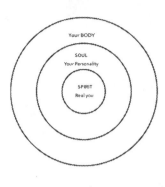

Two pictures of HOMEOSTASIS

These diagrams both illustrate a "whole person." You are not *just* a spirit, you are not *just* a physical body, and you are not *only* a bunch of thoughts and emotions. You *are* a spirit, you *have* a soul, and you *live* in a body. A whole person is a being with these three parts, body, soul, and spirit, which are interconnected and perfectly balanced, as illustrated by these two diagrams.

Like a building, a healthy person has a solid foundation (God's spirit) upon which the rest of the person (body, mind, emotions) depends. This is represented by the pyramid pictured in Diagram A. The foundation, or the bottom of the pyramid, is the strongest part because it supports the rest of the building or person. God designed our "foundation" to be our spirit, not our body, or our mind.

A healthy person also has an inner true self, or core.

This is pictured by concentric circles in Diagram B. The inner core of a person is his or her spirit, from which a person's thoughts, emotions, and body radiate. Your health depends on the health of your inner core. The inner core, your spirit, is like the foundation pictured in the pyramid because everything else about you depends on it.

A person is considered "whole" when his or her body, mind and spirit are in the condition God intended them to be: perfectly balanced and in agreement or at peace with each other. When there is no imbalance of any kind between these three parts of a person, they are said to be in perfect health. In medical terms, this is called, *homeostasis.* According to the Miriam-Webster dictionary, homeostasis is:

(1) The tendency of an organism or a cell to **regulate its internal conditions**, usually by a system of feedback controls, so as to **stabilize health and functioning,** regardless of the outside changing conditions.

(2) The ability of the body or a cell to seek and **maintain a condition of equilibrium or stability within its internal environment** when dealing with external changes.

None of us can achieve absolute perfect homeostasis on our own. We are all born into a sinful world with a sinful nature, therefore, we are all "broken" people; we are *all* off balance! So, how can we develop a foundation or inner core that is healthy and well balanced?

7

The first part of this answer is that we must experience a spiritual birth (see John 3:3-6). This occurs when we seek forgiveness for our sins through the finished work and sacrifice of Jesus Christ on the cross. At that moment, God sends Holy Spirit to live within us and we are now "born again." God designed His perfect Holy Spirit to direct, rule, and control the rest (mind, emotions, and body) of us- in a good way.

If just one of the three parts of us is either over or under active, our whole life becomes off balance. In either case, there is no homeostasis and there is a certain degree of illness. As extreme examples, consider these illustrations:

DIAGRAM C: **DIAGRAM D:**

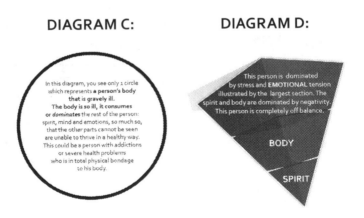

In this diagram, you see only 1 circle which represents **a person's body that is gravely ill.** The body is so ill, it consumes or *dominates* the rest of the person: spirit, mind and emotions, so much so, that the other parts cannot be seen are unable to thrive in a healthy way. This could be a person with addictions or severe health problems who is in total physical bondage to his body.

This person is dominated by stress and **EMOTIONAL** tension illustrated by the largest section. The spirit and body are dominated by negativity. This person is completely off balance.

BODY

SPIRIT

Both the diagram B and C illustrate what a person looks like when one part dominates the others in an unhealthy way.

Jesus said,

> **"But the one who hears my words and**
> **does not put them into practice**
> **is like a man who built a house on the**
> **ground without a foundation."**
> *Luke 6:49 NIV*

The apostle Paul added,

> **For no one can lay any foundation other than**
> **the one already laid, which is Jesus Christ.**
> *1 Corinthians 3:11 NIV*

When your spiritual foundation is broken, off balance, or even non-existent (as in a person who is spiritually "dead" or unregenerate, not born again) it automatically affects the other parts negatively. Your life becomes broken or off balance. Just like a house, your life will eventually collapse.

Why does this happen? Because we are created as *whole* human beings, every part of us is connected to the rest. Just like a building, one part does not exist in isolation from the rest; there is no such thing as independent parts of our person.

For example, a dead or perverted spirit will leave our mind open to distorted thoughts and emotions. A sick mind and toxic emotions will then affect the body negatively. A physical body that is diseased will continue to put more limits on what a person's spirit and mind is fully capable of doing. When one part is affected, the other parts are also affected.

A description of a whole body that needs every part to function properly was used by the apostle Paul to describe the body of Christ in a healthy state:

[12] For as the body is one and has many members, but all the members of that one body, being many, are one body, so also is Christ...[14] For in fact the body [of believers] *is not one member but many.*

[15] If the foot should say, "Because I am not a hand, I am not of the body," is it therefore not of the body? [16] And if the ear should say, "Because I am not an eye, I am not of the body," is it therefore not of the body? [17] If the whole body were an eye, where would be the hearing? If the whole were hearing, where would be the smelling?

[18] But now God has set the members, each one of them, in the body just as He pleased. [19] And if they were all one member, where would the body be? [20] **But now indeed there are many members, yet one body.** *[21] And the eye cannot say to the hand, "I have no need of you"; nor again the head to the feet, "I have no need of you." [22] No, much rather, those members of the body which seem to be weaker are necessary,...*

1 Corinthians 12:12-22 NKJ

The Scripture below describes what happens when one part is dysfunctional:

²⁴ *.... But God composed the body, having given greater honor to that part which lacks it,* ²⁵ ***that there should be no schism*** *[division or separation]* ***in the body,*** *but that the members should have the same care for one another.* ²⁶ ***And if one*** *member [one part of the body]* ***suffers, all the members*** *[parts of the body]* ***suffer with it; or if one member is honored, all the members rejoice with it.***

1 Corinthians 12:24-26 NKJ

When one part of the church does not function properly, the suffering is transferred in one way or another to the rest of the church body. The same thing is true of individuals. So, it is imperative that we have a healthy spirit to rule, or direct our mind and body.

The chain reaction goes something like this*: Your spirit directs or rules your mind, your mind directs your mouth to speak what it thinks, and your body follows what your mouth says.* All of that originates from your spirit and the sum total of whatever it produces is the "real you!"

CH 2: *Becoming the Person That You Want to Be*

So now that you know what the real you is comprised of, do you like you? For many people, this question is a loaded one. We would be surprised to find out how many people just don't like who they are. Many either don't like what they see in themselves, what they feel, what they think, what they have become, or the lives they are living, but they have no idea what to do about it. Many people wish they were something other than what they are. Many people dream about what they wish they were, but never achieve that dream. Maybe this describes you.

Have your hopes and dreams died? Or better yet, have you ever experienced a dream worth living for? Do you wish for a radical change? Are you *ready* to make radical changes in your life? These two concepts, dream and change, go together! You can't have a radical life change without thinking and doing radically different things than you are doing right now. Here is an illustration:

Anyone who has heard stories of wild animals who have grown up in captivity knows that when the time comes for them to be released, they cannot handle the freedom they were created to enjoy. Their natural environment has become unnatural to them. They have to be taught to re-adapt to what should have been normal for them from birth. But somebody thought it would be cute to have them for pets and kept them isolated from their natural environment.

It is a sad thing to watch a TV episode about a wild animal that is afraid of what it is supposed to rule over by nature. The animal has no idea what its life was supposed to be in the wild and instead of embracing its freedom, is full of fear and intimidated by less powerful animals than itself. It can never discover its true identity and abilities as long as it stays in captivity.

Some human beings are in the same condition! They have no idea what or who or where they were created to be. They stay in their familiar little corner of the world because it is the only "safe" thing they know, afraid to venture out. They are living miserable lives, wishing they had *something* worth living for. Or, they are too sick and tired to pursue what they know they want to be. If this describes you, you have been living life "in captivity."

Do you believe that it could be possible that God has something else much better planned for you than what you have experienced? In fact, His plan for all of us *does* include everything that God gave human beings when He originally created them in the Garden of Eden. His plan did *not* include the presence of anything other than what He declared was *good* for us; it did not include depression or oppression. It did not include a life of imbalance and addictions. It *did* and *does* include freedom from the curse of sin, sickness, and death. God's plan for all of us includes living in health and well-being not only because He loves us, but also to reflect Him and to bring Him glory.

Here is just one example of something God planned for and promised you,

> *He* [the Creator] *gives* **power to the weak**,
> *And to those who have no might*
> **He increases strength**...
> *Those who wait in the Lord will* **renew their strength**.
> *They will* **run and not get tired**, **walk and not faint**.
> *Isaiah 40:29, 31 NKJ*

These verses obviously address physical stamina. They comprise a beautiful promise that says you will always have the ability to do whatever you need to do. You might think, "*That sounds nice, but I don't live in an ideal world. I don't think God means literally that I will never get tired.*"

I believe God is speaking about being able to do whatever things you *should* be able to do in this life. You and I are individually created to accomplish whatever we were *meant* to do, and of course, this is different for everyone. But in order to do those things, you have to be physically able.

Do you have energy to do what you were gifted to

do? Are you satisfied with what you know you should be accomplishing, or are you too tired mentally and physically to accomplish what you wish you could do? Do you realize that the condition of your spirit is connected to the condition of your body?

Verses like this were not recorded simply for you to read about what God said to the nation of Israel, and then sit back and admire what happened that one time in history. God had a greater purpose than that when He put together sixty six books over thousands of years that all happen to echo the same message in multiple ways.

Everywhere you look in Scripture, God speaks about energy and strength that proceeds from a right relationship with Him. But somehow, we have missed it. We have depersonalized His promises, and we read them as "nice things that happened in the past to other people."

I refer once again to Diagram A of a "whole "human being. In the circular picture, the inner circle represents the core or the inner most part of you, which is your spirit. It can also be described as your heart. Everything else about you, every other part, revolves around your heart. In other words, the true you is the inner you and everything else you have become and are becoming radiates outward from it. In the New Testament, Jesus said,

> *But those things which **proceed out** of*
> *the mouth **come from the heart***
> *and they defile a man... Matthew 15:18 NKJ*

There are many other Scriptures that support this. Here are a few:

> My **heart** also **instructs** me...
> *Psalm 16:7 NKJ*

> **As a man thinks in his heart, so is he.**
> *Proverbs 23:7 NKJ*

> The **heart is deceitful** above all things and
> desperately wicked; who can know it?
> I, the Lord, search the heart. I test the mind, even to
> give every man according to his ways,
> According to the fruit of his doings.
> *Jeremiah 17:9-10 NKJ*

It is a person's heart that directs his whole being. It is also apparent that by nature, something is wrong with our hearts, according to Jeremiah 17:9-10. As stated earlier, because of our sinful nature, we are born with dysfunctional hearts, and therefore our hearts need redemption. We need new hearts!

When a person's heart is full of negativity, it influences his or her thoughts and emotions negatively. In turn, those thoughts and emotions influence our mouth to speak what we are thinking. And then our body falls in line, receiving its directions from the words we speak. It is a chain reaction.

But God promised to give us a new heart (see Jeremiah chapter 24). And no wonder Jesus said,

He who believes in Me, as the Scripture has said
out of his heart *will flow rivers of living water.*
*But this He spoke **concerning the Spirit**, whom those*
believing in Him would receive...John 7:38-39 NKJ

Jesus knew that we had to have a new heart in order to be made whole again. In fact, one of His favorite questions was, *"Do you wish to be made whole?"* He also said on numerous occasions, *"Your faith has made you whole."* (You can read an example of this in John 5:6-15 KJV.)

If I paraphrase John 7:38-39 above, it would read, *"When your heart completely trusts and believes in Me, you will overflow with the life giving power of My Spirit."*

Notice the end of verse 39 above says that it will be His Holy Spirit that will provide this new life. The source of our wholeness is *His Spirit* flowing out of *our hearts*!

The process of becoming whole is this: we are born again and we receive a new spirit, the Holy Spirit. The Holy Spirit leads our mind, our mind directs our words, and our words direct our body leading to homeostasis.

What is your heart producing? Is it producing health to your mind and your body? Are you bringing forth life giving words? Jesus promises that He will honor whatever is in your heart. When you look at your life right now, it reveals what is in your heart. Do you see the person that you want to be?

Jesus gave us His own peaceful heart:

> **Let not your heart be troubled**, *you*
> *believe in God, believe also in Me...*
> *Peace I leave with you,* **My peace I give to you**.
> **Let not your heart be troubled**, *neither let it be afraid.*
> *John 14:1 & 27 NKJ*

The picture of the pyramid in Diagram A illustrates this concept: the bottom of the structure is its foundation; it is the largest so it can support everything else. *Your heart is your spiritual foundation.* If your heart goes bad, your mind and body goes with it. If the foundation is life giving, the rest of you follows.

> **If our heart condemns us, God is greater**
> **than our heart**, *and knows all things.*
> *Beloved,* **if our heart does not condemn**
> **us, we have confidence** *toward God.*
> *1 John 3:20-21 NKJ*

Is your heart at peace? Where have you placed your confidence and trust? Your physical and mental health are an indication, whether good or bad. Pay attention to what they are telling you!

But don't forget, you have been given the ability to *choose* what your real life will be, starting with the condition of your heart.

CH 3: *Good Health: Your Calling As Christ's Disciple*

In order to fulfill God's plan for your life, you need to be a fully functional disciple of Christ; you need a sound spirit, mind and body. As I present the Scriptures in this chapter, I am asking that you put aside preconceived ideas and prejudices, and take a look at the Bible as an entire unified book.

When one reads any book, one would never think about reading or studying only a few of its chapters and then tell others that you "read" the book and propose to understand what it says. Although I cannot be exhaustive, I can at least present a fair representation of both Old and New Testament teaching on the subject of good health.

I begin this section with the suggestion that the Christian life has been minimized! The master author of compromise himself (the devil) has successfully convinced Christ's followers that there remains only a remnant of what He taught about the kingdom of God left for us today. He has convinced us that our best life on earth is to just hold on and bear with our frustrations until God calls us home. And in many cases, the church has swallowed this lie.

If you are spiritually, mentally, emotionally or physically beaten up and exhausted, your giftedness will be of little or no value. You will be either unable to use your gifts and talents or you will be severely limited in their use, that is why you need good health to live out your calling to represent Christ. I am not speaking about temporary sicknesses that everyone battles because of the presence of toxins around us; I am speaking about a specific dysfunction that defines your life.

In my introduction, I referred to a group of people who could be described as frustrated miracle seekers. They were sure they understood God and prayed in faith, but because they didn't experience the result they desired, they concluded that there must be a problem on God's end. They ended up thinking something like this: *"If I pray and don't experience healing, it must be because God just doesn't heal people miraculously like He did when Jesus walked the earth."*

I have to marvel at this kind of thinking because it assumes God doesn't love or care for people the way He used to, as if He had changed His nature somewhere in time. People who believe that God retired from performing healing miracles today say it is because *"We have the Bible now and we don't need miracles to prove anything else."*

Here's my question: Since when is making people

whole something God does *only* to prove Himself? Jesus was motivated to save us primarily by His *love* for us. Because of that great love, He died to restore what we lost in Garden of Eden, to give us back what He gave mankind in the first place, a state of complete well-being that lasts forever. He redeemed us because He loves us and wants the best for His people *at all times*, just like any good parent would want the best for their children *at all times*.

If your children get sick, how do you respond? If they get ill, do you say, *"Good! You'll become a better person!"?* Do you think or respond that way? Even though we know our children can certainly learn something from *any* situation, good or bad, we don't *wish* them to get and stay sick, and neither does God. If that *was* the case, then we should *help* them stay sick! And for heaven's sake, then we shouldn't give them medicine or ever take them to the doctor! That would be contrary to the goal of helping them become a better person.

That is terrible logic, not to mention cruel. The fact is you or I will always help our sick children get better as fast as possible. We would never purposely inflict or encourage sickness to stay in their lives. So, why would we think it is God's nature to leave us in the same kind of state? It is completely contrary to His loving nature.

I have encountered Christians who stare at me blankly if I even so much as suggest that they could pray and seek God's perspective about their situation *before* they took any medication or saw a doctor about their condition. Please understand, I do not devalue the use of medical options; I just suggest we go to God *first.* This seems to be a foreign idea to many people.

I have also noticed that it is usually the same people who ascribe to the above thinking almost always *also* subscribe to the belief that the Word of God must be interpreted properly and has the final authority in their lives. They attest strongly to living their lives by it. However, in testifying to the importance of the Bible, they have also missed a good portion of its teaching on this subject of health.

I would like to unpack the error in this type of thinking using the very word of God many profess to believe, but we must look at the Bible *in its entirety*, Old and New Testament. They are a part of the same book.

While it is impossible to cover this *entire* subject in one small book, I will start with an example in the book of Proverbs, where we are told that obeying God's words will keep us in good health:

My son, give attention to **My words;**
Incline your ear to my sayings.
Do not let them depart from your eyes;
Keep them in the midst of your heart;
For they are life to those who find them
and health to all their flesh.
Proverbs 4:20-22 NKJ

These verses are very clear. God says that good health *to our flesh,* in other words, to our body, has everything to do with obedience to His words. It is stated clearly as it could possibly be stated in these verses.

Now, let's go to the New Testament and examine the main directive given by Jesus to His church as it also relates to health and well-being.

> *And as you go, preach, saying, 'The*
> *kingdom of heaven is at hand.'*
> **Heal the sick, cleanse the lepers, raise**
> **the dead, cast out demons.**
> *Freely you have received, freely give.*
> *Matthew 10:7-8 NKJ*

It might seem odd to you to equate the mission of the church with instructions about restoring health, however, these are the words Jesus spoke and He linked these concepts together. Jesus must have had a reason for putting all these things together in one command. I propose that it is because the gospel message is one that affects the *entire* life of a person, and therefore it must be presented in its fullness.

Many people reading the above Scripture verses today would ignore the middle line of these verses. They would say that we are to preach about the kingdom of heaven and give freely, but it ends there. They would say that healing the sick, casting out demons and raising the dead is not needed by today's church, and that Jesus was only talking to His disciples at that time. Those who say this are usually the same people who say that they live their lives by the word of God. If God loves us the same today as He did then, and if He is the same God He was at that time, then a number of questions about this perspective arise.

The first and most obvious question is this: *"Was there any greater need for healing, deliverance from demons, or living a full life (without premature death) in Jesus' day than there is now? Have we come to a place where the medical profession can fix everything without God's help?"*

It doesn't take much to answer that question honestly with a resounding, "No." We can see by reading the newspaper and watching the news that people are walking around today with the same sins and sicknesses that were recorded in the Bible; human nature still has the same problems. People still commit adultery, they have relationship conflicts, their family members get sick, etc. To argue that point would be like arguing that the sky used to be blue but is not blue anymore.

Second question: *"If it was true, that somehow there was a greater need for people to experience healing, deliverance, and living a complete mature life in Jesus' day than there is today, how much of the rest of Jesus' teachings applies only to His day and not to our lifetime?"*

Third question: *"If it is true that some of His teachings were only for that time, which ones do we ignore and which ones do we keep? And what is the standard we will use to know which teachings we should keep and which to ignore? How would we know?"* This question would demand an answer from a select few who would be designated as "qualified" to make such decisions based purely on their own subjective judgments.

Needless to say, subjective judgments would then open the door to a high degree of disagreement because many different beliefs would abound. We would have many "versions" of Scripture. Confusion would reign because no one would know for sure what gets tossed out and what doesn't. Does that sound remotely like anything going on today? An obvious answer would have to be, "Yes."

There is another popular passage known as the Great Commission. This command is considered a major mission or function of the church. In other words, it is for the whole church for all time. Evangelism, missions and discipleship are the focus of the church for all time because of this command:

And Jesus came and spoke to them, saying,
"All authority has been given to Me
in heaven and on earth.
Go therefore and make disciples *of all the nations,*
baptizing them in the name of the Father
and of the Son and of the Holy Spirit,
teaching them to observe all things
that I have commanded you;...
Matthew 28:18-20 NKJ

I can't help but notice that last line. Jesus said we are to teach converts to observe all of the things He commanded them. *All* things He commanded? Did He make a distinction? Would that also include all of Matthew chapter 10:7 and 8, to heal the sick, deliver from demons and raise the dead? That command to make disciples is the main task of the church, and we are to follow it just the way Jesus taught it until He returns so that we can accurately represent Him!

I also can't imagine that Jesus had a timeline in mind when He spoke these things. I am sure it was not His intent to imply, *"Teach them all the things I have commanded you until 'X" time. After 'X' amount of years go by, preach only about the kingdom of God because then there will be no need to heal the sick or cast out demons."*

It is interesting to note that in the command to make disciples in Matthew 10:7-8, Jesus includes His explanation of what this would look like. People would be freed from illnesses. They would be freed from demonic influence. Their skin diseases would be healed. Those that experienced premature death would be freed from that also!

And why would He lump these things together following His command to preach that the kingdom of God is at hand? What do they have to do with salvation process? They have to do with restoring a *whole* person, not just one spiritual part!

The only way to bypass the entirety of this command is to also toss out much of the rest of the gospels and New Testament. So much of it includes salvation that happened alongside miracles, healing, and deliverance, and there is a very good reason why. It has to do with the accurate meaning of the word "salvation," or "save." This is explained in the next chapter.

CH 4: *The Real Meaning of "Saved"*

The word "save" in its original Greek language is the word, "sozo". The definition of this word is as follows:

SOZO: safe and sound, to rescue from danger or destruction (from injury or peril)
> A. to save a suffering one (from perishing), i.e. one suffering from disease, to make well, heal, restore to health
> B. to preserve one who is in danger of destruction, to save or rescue

Here are three verses in the New Testament that use this word:

1. *"That if you confess with your mouth Jesus is Lord and believe in your heart that God raised Him from the dead you shall be **saved (sozo)."** Romans 10:9 NKJ*

2. *"But Jesus turning and seeing her said 'Daughter take courage your faith has **made** you **well (sozo) [KJ:***

whole] *and at once the woman was* **made well (sozo)** **[KJ: whole]."** *Matthew 9:22 KJV*

3. *"And those who had seen it reported to them how the man who was demon-possessed had been* **made well (sozo) [KJ: healed]."** *Luke 8:36 KJV*

In all three of these verses, the same word, *sozo*, is used. But each passage speaks about a different aspect of it. The first one is about confessing salvation, the second is about physically healing and the third one is demonic deliverance. But they all use the *same word!*

The clear implication is this: that when a person is saved, it means they are not only *healed "spiritually"*, but it means they are given freedom from all the curses of sickness that go with it.[1]

"To save, heal and deliver" is an expression *of one and the same concept.* Simply putting these words together, you are able to get the whole picture. To be "saved" means to be saved, healed, delivered, preserved, protected, to be made prosperous and whole. The word "whole" means complete, or that nothing is missing and nothing is broken."[2]

Does that change your understanding of what Jesus intended when He asked us to preach the gospel? He never intended us to pull apart the whole concept of salvation and preach only the spiritual part of it; He intended us to first become "whole" individuals (saved) and then to go and make more whole individuals. He intended us to reproduce our own kind! That is the meaning of "preach the kingdom of God," the business to which we are to be about.

If ever you are to convince someone of the truth, you must experience that truth yourself first, otherwise you will be called a liar. Would you ever want to do business with a salesperson that comes to your door trying to sell you something that he or she declines to use? I wouldn't. My first question would be, *"How do you yourself like this product? Do you use it? Do you own one?"* If the answer is *"No,"* then I have no further interest in either this salesperson or the item they are attempting to sell me. I know that person is not really convinced of the value of the item they are selling because they were not willing to experience it themselves. Do we expect the Christian life to be any different?

As Christians, should we sell "fire insurance "*only?* We tell people, *"You need salvation to prepare for your next life,"* which is true, and eternally important, of course. But, did Jesus approach mankind with a message about the future alone? Did He save people's sins and leave them sick and oppressed by demons?

No, His message was, "You can be free from sin *now, and* for eternity. You can get rid of those demons *right now.* You can be assured of finding the reason you were created without worrying about whether you will live to accomplish it." (This is my paraphrase of Matthew 10:7-8). Jesus came to repair what was broken in our lives *in the present time* as well as give people hope for the future! He wanted to restore His original plan for each one of our lives on the earth now, *as well as* our future in heaven.

Look at the way He taught us to pray:

> *Our Father in heaven, Hallowed be*
> *Your name. Your kingdom come.*
> **Your will be done on earth as it is in heaven**.
> *Matthew 6:9b-10 NKJ*

Jesus' mission is to bring His kingdom back to the earth as it was before the fall and He passed that mission on to us. His prayer speaks of the kingdom He has prepared for us from the beginning. He wants us to be a part of it now on earth, not just later when we die. His prayer has definite implications for our lives on earth from the moment we decide to receive forgiveness and become "wholly saved."

CH 5: *The "Whole" Gospel*

Usually, when we get physically sick, we enlist the help of a medical doctor who is educated and trained to treat one thing: our body. He or she has not studied how a person's mind and spirit operate. And so he or she treats only the body, without much, if any, regard to what is going on in the rest of our person. Sometimes it works, sometimes it doesn't. Many times it works temporarily, and sometimes not at all.

If a person has a mental or emotional problem, that person will usually seek out a counselor of some sort, or a psychologist or a psychiatrist. These doctors are educated and trained to treat one part of you: your mind and emotions. In comparison to medical doctors, they have studied *little* about the body. Typically, psychologists and psychiatrists do not also have knowledge or training to include spiritual intervention in their treatment, which may very well be needed in order to treat a person's mental problem.

When people have spiritual problems, guess who

they go to? They go to their pastor, priest, or rabbi who is taught in one area: spiritual knowledge.

None of these three types of professionals typically know or apply much about the other two areas in their treatments. By now, you realize that we are talking about holistic treatment, also known as holistic medicine.

There are lots of holistic or homeopathic doctors around. Many of those that you see advertised use man-centered spiritual teaching in their field of expertise, also known by terms such as *new age,* or *humanism.* That means they use research and knowledge gained from the experiences of other people and the *opinions* of these people.

If you haven't already noticed, there is a *vast* amount of disagreement when it comes to these doctors. Why? Because they do not have *one reliable source of spiritual information.* They have to reference all kinds of books with all kinds of philosophies written by a whole bunch of imperfect people who have their own limited spiritual ideas, all of which conflict at some point. We can expect that kind of conflict among health professionals, because they are imperfect human people who lack knowledge of all the truth that exists. Only One Person knows everything that can be known, and that is God Himself.

So, if we cannot rely on any of these doctors who are lacking in some knowledge or other, who *do* we rely on and where do we go for help? I'd like to suggest we go to the One Person who knows everything about every one of us, how we were made down to most intricate detail about us, including how many hairs are on our head. He created every part of us; so of course, He *knows* how every part of us works, spirit, soul and body! Shouldn't He be the One we go to for first for wisdom and understanding that helps us become the person we were meant to be?

That One Person also wrote a book so that He could pass on all the information we needed to know in order to be whole. That book is the Bible, which is given to us for every need we will encounter in this life, not only spiritual, but also physical, mental, and emotional, as well as other areas.

The seed of the whole gospel was presented by God directly to His own people in Old Testament days. God essentially gave his people, the nation of Israel, the same instructions that Jesus gave his disciples in Matthew 10:7 and 8; they were to preach and obey the laws of His kingdom and they could expect to live healthy prosperous lives so that they would be able to serve Him fully and completely.

God gave His people strict laws about health that were connected to spiritual or moral laws. When we read the book of Leviticus, which includes instructions to the priests, the word, "holy" is used over and over. There were laws for sanctification, holiness, or purity that represented God's own nature, which is holy or "clean."

From the beginning, God desired His own people to be different, or separated from other nations for this purpose of serving Him, representing Him and enjoying their own well-being. There were laws for clean living, clean animals, clean land, etc. You can read about foods that were allowed and forbidden by God (for health reasons) in Leviticus chapter 11.

In Leviticus, chapter 13, we read instructions for people who had leprosy, or a variety of skin diseases. The interesting thing is that there is no mention of physicians in this book. God's people were expected to follow all His instructions for good health and the people who had the authority to oversee that they did were priests, not doctors. When they had a problem, they were instructed to go to the men of God; in today's language, that would be pastors or elders. Here is an example,

[2] *"When a man has on the skin of his body a swelling, a scab, or a bright spot, and it becomes on the skin of his body like a leprous **sore**[3] [Hebrew: [3]**saraath, disfiguring skin diseases**], then he shall be brought to Aaron the priest or to one of his sons the priests.* [3] **The priest shall examine the sore on the skin of the body**; *and if the hair on the sore has turned white, and the sore appears to be deeper than the skin of his body, it is a leprous sore.* **Then the priest shall examine him, and pronounce him unclean**. *Leviticus 13:2-3 NKJ*

In verses 47-51 there are further instructions about contagious disease:

"As for any fabric that is spoiled with a defiling mold [**fungus, or similar infestation**] *any woolen or linen*

clothing ⁴⁸ *any woven or knitted material of linen or wool, any leather or anything made of leather—* ⁴⁹ *if the affected area in the fabric, the leather, the woven or knitted material, or any leather article, is greenish or reddish, it is a defiling mold and* **must be shown to the priest.** ⁵⁰ **The priest is to examine the affected area and isolate the article for seven days.** ⁵¹ **On the seventh day he is to examine it,** *and if the mold has spread in the fabric, the woven or knitted material, or the leather, whatever its use, it is a persistent defiling mold; the article is unclean." Leviticus 13:47-51 NIV*

The priests had God's authority to pronounce a person sick or well. The spiritual leaders were the doctors of the day; God appointed them to diagnose illness or wellness. The people were given strict dietary laws concerning clean and unclean animals that they were permitted or not permitted to eat (see Leviticus chapter 11), all for their health and well-being. The priests were responsible to teach and enforce these laws, not doctors.

Since God gave strict instructions to His people from the very beginning concerning food, we need to recognize that these principles still apply to a great degree today. The make up of our bodies has not changed. Yet, much of our food today has been diluted, polluted, and processed. We have produced flawed food sources depleted of essential nutrients that God created for perfect health.

We have substituted and consume food laden with

chemicals (hormones, pesticides, artificial colors and artificial vitamins, etc.) for food in its natural state. The more we use unnatural and inorganic chemicals to grow our plants and feed our animals the more chemical imbalance and disease can thrive in our bodies.

God never intended for farmers to use toxic poisons to control disease, genetically alter our food, or substitute "fake" junk foods for the real thing.

Doing these things to our plants and animals is also a form of rebellion against God's perfect creation! We can't continue to consume these products on a regular basis and then also expect to enjoy long term health!

Back in Exodus chapter 15, God gives this promise to Moses to declare to His people,

*If you diligently heed the voice of the LORD your God and do what is right in His sight, give ear to His commandments and keep all His statutes**, I will put none of the diseases on you which I have brought on the Egyptians for I am the LORD who heals you**."*
Exodus 15:26 NKJ

and then again in chapter 23:

[25] "So you shall serve the LORD your God, and He will bless your bread and your water [food and drink]. *And I will take sickness away from the midst of you. [26] No one shall suffer miscarriage or be barren in your land; I will fulfill the number of your days. Exodus 23:25-6 NKJ*

What wonderful promises! God says if His people obey all His principles, they will enjoy a life free of sickness and disease. Not only that, but they will live a full life and not die prematurely!

In Deuteronomy chapter 28, God gives an *extensive* list of all the sicknesses that will come upon His people if they *fail* to obey his spiritual and dietary laws. Just some of those diseases include: fevers, inflammation, plagues of all kinds, tumors, sores, skin diseases, and confusion of the mind including insanity. All of these diseases are in existence today. He ends the chapter by saying,

58 **"If you do not carefully observe all the words of this law that are written in this book,** *that you may fear this glorious and awesome name, THE LORD YOUR GOD,* *59* **then the Lord will bring upon you and your descendants extraordinary plagues**-*great and prolonged plagues-and* **serious and prolonged sicknesses**. *60Moreover He will bring back on you all the* **diseases** *of Egypt, of which you were afraid, and* **they shall cling to you.** *61* **Also every sickness and every plague, which is not written in this Book** *of the Law, will the Lord bring upon you until you are destroyed. Deuteronomy 28:58-61 NKJ*

What does this mean? From the beginning, God is our source of life and health. He warned us in the above passages that our physical lives would reflect our spiritual condition. If obedience to God declines, physical and mental health also declines. The more we substitute anything else (our "idols") for a right relationship with God, the more off balance or sick we will be.

Why don't we hear about these things more often? What we have done is substitute a partial and disconnected gospel for the "whole gospel!" The whole gospel is good news to our soul, spirit *and body*, but we have removed much from the salvation (sozo) experience and have focused only on the moral part.

When we receive salvation, we should be receiving and experiencing the process of spiritual restoration, but we should *also* experience mental, emotional, and physical wellness, financial freedom (see 3 John 2) wisdom and understanding (see Proverbs 1:7) and a character makeover (see Galatians 5:22-3)!

Here is another description of benefits we are to receive with salvation:

Bless the LORD, O my soul;
And all that is within me, *bless* His holy name!
² Bless the LORD, O my soul, and
forget not *all His benefits*:
³ Who *forgives all your iniquities*,
who *heals all your diseases*,
⁴ Who **redeems your life** from destruction,
Who crowns you with **lovingkindness
and tender mercies**,

⁵ Who **satisfies** your mouth with good *things*,
So that your **youth is renewed** like the eagle's.
Psalm 103:1-5 NKJ

Now that's a description of wholeness and restoration! God has given us back all the things we lost in the fall of man, but we have not preached the whole message; we have only preached the spirit part of it!

You might say, "*I know non-Christians who are in good health and they are not saved (sozo), what about that?*" That is because God's principles for health work for whoever follows them, whether they call themselves Christians or not! I don't know about you, but why would I choose only to receive part of God's benefits when I can experience all of what God desires for me?

CH 6: *The Spirit Leads*

In chapter 1, we discussed the real you and how God created you as a three part being. A person's spirit is the core of who they are; therefore, your mind, emotions and body are the external manifestations of what is going on inside the real you, the spiritual you.

Here is a quick test question: What part of you has supreme authority in your life right now? Are you ruled by your spirit? Do your emotions rule your life? Or does your body dictate most decisions?

Only you can answer that question honestly. You will know the answer by observing your current condition. If you can honestly answer that you are at peace with God, yourself and others, and you enjoy good health most of the time, you are predominantly spirit-controlled. If you are battling either a controlling mental or physical problem that significantly interferes with most of your daily decisions, there is hope for something better.

In a circumstance where you have experienced a physical handicap due to an injury or accident, you obviously cannot control your present condition and you are in a unique situation. Outside of a re-creative miracle, God may have a specific plan for your condition which includes using it for His special purposes. But even though that may be true, you do not have to be bound by a dysfunctional spirit or mind. You can still overcome your disability to a great degree even in your apparent physical limitation.

For example, you may have heard of the following true life story of a man born with only a torso and no limbs:

Nick Vujicic was born in 1982 without arms and legs. The Vujicic family refused to allow his physical condition to limit his lifestyle.

Since his first speaking engagement at age 19, Nick has traveled around the world, sharing his story with millions. Today this dynamic young evangelist has accomplished more than most people achieve in a lifetime. He's an author, musician, actor, and his hobbies include fishing, painting and swimming. Nick is the president of the international non-profit ministry, Life Without Limbs, which was established in 2005.

Nick says, "If God can use a man without arms and legs to be His hands and feet, then He will certainly use any willing heart!"[3]

This man's life is nothing short of miraculous. But chronic and continual illness of either mind or body is different; it is a signal that your inner spirit is also "sick" in some way.

It could just be that you have willfully ignored basic good health habits, such as a healthy diet, adequate sleep, and a peaceful lifestyle, but this is *also* a spiritual problem. Any time you ignore good stewardship of your body, it is an indicator God's priorities are not your priorities, in other words: it is disobedience. A disobedient inner spirit is a sick one.

Many people *think* they are living an obedient healthy lifestyle, but in reality they have no idea what that really is. As I mentioned previously, because almost all of our foods have been genetically altered, polluted or processed in some way, and our air, water and atmosphere is also polluted, there will always be a certain amount of disease that will continually influence us. However, we can exercise control over *how much* these things control us, and with God's instructions, we can even eventually overcome these obstacles to a great degree.

If you care about your spiritual condition, you automatically will care about your physical condition, and therefore you also need to know what real food or "whole food" is. As stated previously, food that has been altered from the way God created it is not what our bodies were created to consume. We were not created to eat artificial fruit substitutes like jello, or fake foods such as hydrogenated oil, which has basically removed all the nutrients and leaves only empty fat calories.

Since this is not a cookbook or medical book, I am not going to explain this in any more depth. Anyone who wishes to know more on this subject can find much information on the internet; it is loaded with information about the subject of "whole food," or food that has not been processed in any way.

As discussed previously, your spirit (good or bad) leads your mind, thoughts and emotions, your mind directs your words and your words direct your body to action. You might ask, *"How can I become intentional about that?"*

You have already begun by recognizing that your spirit is the source of who you really are. If you have received Christ as your *personal* Lord and Savior (not just acknowledge who He is, but you have entered into a personal relationship with Him) you have already completed the first step. The real you is no longer spiritually dead, but alive in Christ!

The second step is to read and learn God's instructions in His word, the Bible. You cannot expect direction in your spirit from God if you have no idea what guidelines He has already put in place!

Third, acknowledge the presence of the Holy Spirit and welcome His leading in *every aspect* of your life. God's spirit was given to you as your Counselor and Helper. He is the one who renews your life, your spirit, your mind and your body.

If you want to improve yourself, then you must learn to recognize the ways He leads. Your natural mind will fight this. You will want to reason your way through each situation, which by nature opposes what the Spirit wants to do. Begin to recognize and reject your old "default" thinking!

When there is a conflict between your mind and your spirit, you will feel uncomfortable and insecure. Your will says, *"I want to do what is comfortable and familiar,"* and at the same time, the Holy Spirit will be showing you something new and different. Your natural mind does not like to submit to anything it can't control, but remember, when you came into a relationship with your *Lord, He* is now your Lord, not you! You are going to have to make a choice to do some uncomfortable things.

You want radical change? Make a decision to do radically different things! Decide to train yourself to trust the Holy Spirit's leading. Here is a passage of Scripture that outlines ways He will help you:

> [9] *But as it is written:" Eye has not seen, nor ear heard,*
> *Nor have entered into the heart of man*
> *The things which God has prepared*
> *for those who love Him."*
> [10] **But God has revealed them to**
> **us through His Spirit.**
> **For the Spirit searches all things,**
> *yes, the deep things of God.*
> [11] *For what man knows the things of a man*
> *except the spirit of the man which is in him?*
> **Even so no one knows the things of**
> **God except the Spirit of God.**
> [12] *Now we have received, not the spirit of the world,*
> *but the Spirit who is from God, that*
> *we might know the things that*
> *have been freely given to us by God.*
> [13] *These things we also speak,* **not in words**
> **which man's wisdom teaches**

> *but which the Holy Spirit teaches,*
> *comparing spiritual things with spiritual.*
> **14 But the natural man does not receive**
> **the things of the Spirit of God,**
> **for they are foolishness to him;**
> **nor can he know them,**
> **because they are spiritually discerned***...*
> *But we have the mind of Christ.*
> *1 Corinthians 2: 9-16 NKJ*

Did you catch all those verbs? The Holy Spirit will *reveal things to you, search all things for you, will teach you all things, and give you knowledge and discernment.* These things are His responsibility concerning you! Are you teachable? Is your mind and heart open to what He is showing you?

If your answer is "*Yes,*" that means you need to invite Him into every situation you encounter and ask Him to show you what you need to know. Praying becomes of utmost importance (see Ephesians 6:18) if you want to *hear* from the Holy Spirit. Here are steps to let the Spirit of God lead you in all things:

1.   **Clear your mind.** Get in a quiet place with God without interruptions. Turn off your cell phone and don't answer the door. Put aside any preconceived ideas and thoughts and ideas.
2.   **Pray** *first. Before* you do anything else. Ask the Holy Spirit to speak clearly to you and to help you hear clearly concerning your situation.

3. **Check in with God's word.** What, if any, directions are given in God's Word concerning your situation? Is there anything you have overlooked or intentionally ignored?

4. **Ask God for His agenda and His priorities** concerning your spiritual, mental, emotional and physical health. Do they line up with *your* agenda and priorities?

5. **Wait until you have heard from God clearly**, then make a change, not before.

6. **Don't delay to obey.** When you know what you should do, but don't do it—it is sin! (James 4:17) Obey quickly.

Sometimes, your spirit will sense something before your mind comprehends it. By nature, you may feel "uncomfortable" with what you are sensing spiritually. *But this is the defining moment of knowing how to let the spirit lead.* Eventually, the truth will be revealed to your mind as well, but it may take longer to "catch up" with your spirit. Don't bail out on the Holy Spirit just because your mind disagrees with His prompting! Give Him a chance to show you what He wants to do!

Be encouraged:

> *But the natural man does not receive the things of the Spirit of God, for they are foolishness to him; nor can he know them, because **they are spiritually discerned**.*
> *1 Corinthians 2:14 NKJ*

> [18] *while we **do not look at the things which are
> seen**, but at the things which are not seen.
> For the things which are seen are temporary, but
> the **things which are not seen are eternal**.*
> *2 Corinthians 4:18 NKJ*

Remember, your natural way of thinking is changing. Your job is to prepare yourself to welcome and receive all the insight the Holy Spirit gives when He leads you.

CH 7: *Renewing and Guarding Your Mind and Emotions*

As Christians, our goal is not only to be "spiritually saved," but to be "made whole." We must include our mind and emotions in the salvation process.

If I am born again with a new spirit, if I eat all the right things, get plenty of rest and a fair amount of exercise, and yet my thoughts and emotions remain toxic, all the good things I do amount to nothing! I will sabotage my health and cancel out all the good habits by failing to change the negative junk going on inside my head and heart.

What is the evidence of toxic thoughts and emotions? Here is the indicator: Do you experience inner peace and joy *most of the time, some of the time, or never?* Your answer is the degree of your mental and emotional health.

Achieving good health requires mental and emotional peace in all situations. Until you have achieved that, your body will act as if it is at war with itself, manifested by illness. Have you ever had this thought, *"It seems like my body is my worst enemy!"*? I know I have. It was at the worst point of my own illness that I had this epiphany: *"My body is at war with me—and it is because of my emotions!"* I had to admit that I had deep seated resentment towards some family members and even my own *self!* I had to get alone with God and get His help to cleanse my heart of unforgiveness and self-righteous resentment.

Okay, so you admit, *"I have emotional issues."* Maybe it's a problem with fear or anxiety, maybe you feel depressed, or maybe you struggle with anger or bitterness. Whatever the negative emotion, there is a spiritual problem fueling these emotions, and these in turn produce chemical imbalances in the body which can cause disease. Emotional issues are really "heart" issues. Our hearts carry our deepest emotions, so we need to do a constant heart check up.

The first thing to do is find the source and examine it. For example, if you have been offended, you must forgive and be reconciled to God and to the third party, if possible. If it is not possible that the party that offended you will cooperate or perhaps is not alive today, you go to God and ask Him to help you forgive, and then you have done all of your part. You then release that emotional "poison" and let it "drain from your brain"! You let God take care of the consequences both for you and that party that offended you. If you don't, you have opened your body up to all kinds of diseases that proceed from bitterness. Here are a few documented ones:

Angina, anorexia, asthma, arthritis, bladder, bowel and back problems, cancers, fibromyalgia, crones disease, eczema, epilepsy, heart problems, hernias, hives, multiple sclerosis, migraines, paranoia, rashes, seizures, sleep apnea, schizophrenia, strokes, ulcers...[4]

These are only a few, and they are examples of what toxic emotions do to our bodies with the chemicals they create. I am not saying these diseases are *always* caused by emotions, but much of the time they are. They can also be caused by other imbalances such as poor nutrition, over medication, exposure to pollution, traumatic events, etc. Whatever the cause, they can eventually be corrected, if you are willing to start the process!

If you are angry at circumstances that you cannot control, again, go to God and remind yourself that His plan for you is perfect and *will never ever change,* no matter what your circumstance appears to be at the moment (see Jeremiah 29:11). There are many ways God can accomplish what He wants in your life; many paths can lead you to the place that is right for you! He is not limited by circumstances, by your failures, your past mistakes or by things or people that hurt you in the past. As you read the Old and New Testament, see how many flawed men and women were used in mighty ways by God!

If fear and intimidation is your issue, you must begin to see yourself as God created you in Christ Jesus and receive what He has died to give you. Fear is a sign of either ignorance of what God has done for you, or of prideful immaturity which refuses to receive God's provision. It manifests in the form of anxieties of many different kinds. It is failure to trust and believe that God really loves you enough:

> ***There is no fear in love; but perfect
> love casts out fear,***
> *because fear involves torment.*
> But ***he who fears has not been made perfect in love.***
> *1 John 4:18 NKJ*

You will need to build "a fortress," or a wall, around your mind in order to protect yourself from absorbing wrong thinking into your body. How do you build this guard wall around your mind?

First, your mind must be renewed (see Romans 12:1-2). If you aren't reading God's words and being comforted by them, how will you know what your thoughts should be? That is first. Spend time reading the Bible; get to know what it says because these are God's words *to you.* You can't build a guard around your mind if you have no truths from which to build it. Every thought you have must be directed by what you know is true, and if it is not, reject it!

> ...**casting down arguments** and every high thing
> that exalts itself against the knowledge of God,
> **bringing every thought into captivity
> to the obedience of Christ**,...
> *2 Corinthians 10:5 NKJ*

When your thoughts are brought into captivity, they are ruled or dominated by something else. What should rule the thoughts in your mind? Your spirit is designed by God to rule your mind, and this a good thing!

The Holy Spirit is a good master, kind, compassionate, loving and patient, so He can teach you to be patient with yourself while you train your mind to obey your renewed spirit!

CH 8: *Your Mind Directs Your Mouth and Your Mouth Directs Your Body*

Going back to the passage in the first chapter of Corinthians we read:

> **These things we also speak, not in words which man's wisdom teaches but which the Holy Spirit teaches**, *comparing spiritual things with spiritual.*
> *1 Corinthians 2:13 NKJ*

Do you understand what this is saying? When your mind has learned how to take directions from your spirit (the Holy Spirit), the next step is to let your mouth take directions from your renewed mind.

Your words are already a product of agreement with your thoughts, and they either produce health, or they remove it:

> *A man's stomach shall be satisfied from the fruit of his mouth;*

> **From the produce of his lips he shall be filled.**
> **Death and life are in the power of the tongue,**
> *And those who love it will eat its fruit.*
> *Proverbs 18:20-21 NKJ*

Either way, good or bad, your body responds to the words that come out of your mouth. It is already happening, whether you know it or not.

What is your state of overall well-being? I'm not talking about the occasional cold, etc. Everyone experiences an attack of illness now and then. Don't confuse an attack with defeat. But if you are in constant and continual state of pain, discomfort, or illness *without improvement*, you need to do a spirit-mind-mouth check up to find out what is off balance.

Are you quenching the spirit somewhere? Is your mind at constant odds with the Holy Spirit? Are your words contrary to what God says about you? Are you ignoring health habits that you know to be right? Your body is already following what *you* have been telling it to do!

Again, I am not talking about momentary or temporary physical attacks; they will come because we all live in a broken fallen world. I am talking about a constant state of illness that owns and defines your life.

Some examples of symptoms might be: constant digestion issues such as IBS, constant allergies, constant inflammation that causes constant pain, constant high blood pressure, constant emotional agitation, depression, and addictions of any kind. Notice, I say "constant" with all of these indicators because we can all be affected temporarily at some point or another.

Remember that God's word does not work in isolation. It must permeate our whole life in order to bring back the perfectly balanced condition we were originally created to enjoy. Speaking all the right words won't do a bit of good if we are disobedient to God's health principles at the same time! Don't go to the altar and get anointed with oil and prayed over for healing if you have every intention of continuing poor health habits!

If you have no idea where your physical problem originates, you need to open yourself up to a Holy Spirit search. Ask Him to show you where the disconnect lies. Perhaps your heart is hurting and you need to do battle with forgiveness. Remember those Scriptures about the heart? Whatever is in there comes out in your emotions, your words, and your body!

Perhaps you have an addiction of some kind. Addictions are a sign that you are filling a God shaped void in your life with something else that has taken His place and has become your idol. Perhaps you are overbooked and stressed out trying to accomplish something that God never intended for you. Allow the Holy Spirit to come in and shine the light on the places you have kept closed off in self-defense for so long. God can heal every broken place in your life, but you must give Him *access* to them first! He will never come in against your will.

If you are pondering whether you can trust Him, He is a trustworthy and faithful God who only has good things in mind for you! (see Jeremiah 29:11)

Whatever you think, you will speak. Jesus said that we speak from the overflow of what is inside of us (our heart). Whatever is inside you will eventually come out, one way or another:

> *"But those **things which proceed out of the mouth** come from the heart and they **defile a man**..." Matthew 15:18 NKJ*

If you don't like what you hear yourself saying and you don't like what you see in yourself, you have been given the choice and the ability to change it. God offers you His Spirit and His ability to make whatever change you need; He offers you a chance to partake of His divine nature! (see 2 Peter 1:4).

Your spirit must now begin training your mind. Every time you think something contrary to what builds you up, every time you think something opposed to what God says about you in His word, you must reign in your wayward thoughts. You must replace the old thinking with new thoughts and your language will automatically change as a result. Your mind directs your mouth! The following is a quote from a blog so beautifully expressed by Matthew McDonald:

*"There are moments in our walk with God that we do feel weak; we feel inadequate...**Keep saying in faith, "I am strong in the Lord and the power of his might! "Let the weak say, "I am strong."** (Joel 3:10 NKJ)*

Week by week, and then day by day, that mountain will get smaller and smaller as the word of God in you grows bigger and bigger, that it will overcome! It will prevail! The word of God will roar mightily, "By the stripes of Jesus I am healed, I am an overcomer!"[5]

Your words are either life giving or death producing. The condition of your body has a direct correlation to the things you say about yourself, circumstances, and others. Remember, our body was designed to move in concert with our soul and spirit, so that is what it does. Your body *follows* your speech. Change your speech, change the way your body acts.

CH 9: *Do You Want to Be Made Whole?*

As stated before, Jesus speaks of salvation interchangeably with a person's wellness or wholeness. He stated clearly what His mission on earth was:

> For the Son of Man has come to seek and to save [sozo: heal, deliver] that which was lost."
> Luke 19:10 NKJ

Here is another instance:

> [16] And when the scribes and Pharisees saw Him eating with the tax collectors and sinners, they said to His disciples,
> "How is it that He eats and drinks with tax collectors and sinners?"
> [17] When Jesus heard it, He said to them,
> **"Those who are well* have no need of a physician, but those who are sick.**

> ### *I did not come to call the righteous,*
> ### *but sinners, to repentance."*
> #### *Mark 2:16-17 NKJ*

In the Old King James, verse 17 reads, *"Those who are *whole have no need of the physician..."* In either translation, "well" or "whole," the same Greek word *ischuo* is used, meaning *to be able, avail, might, prevail, strength*.

Clearly, the Greek translation of this word refers to a physical state of being; those who are able bodied have no need of help. But Jesus uses this same word interchangeably as He refers to the *spiritual* condition of the needy.

The Greek word for "sick" in this passage is *kakos*, meaning *worthless, depraved, bad, evil*, and *diseased*. In this instance, unlike other passages that speak specifically and *only* about *physically* sick people, Jesus uses one word to include *two* different conditions, physical *and* spiritual, simultaneously.

If we were to translate the exact meaning of these words in English, the verse would read, *"Those who are able and strong have no need of a physician, but those who feel worthless, depraved, bad, evil, and diseased."* That gives a little more insight into this statement.

If we translate Jesus' second statement, *"I did not call the righteous, but sinners to repentance,"* we could say, *"I did not call those who are not depraved, evil or have no diseases to repent, but those that are sick."*

Jesus connects the mental and physical condition to the spiritual condition of the heart.

One of the most famous passages that you may hear quoted about physical healing is this one:

> *Surely he hath **borne our griefs,***
> ***and carried our sorrows***:
> *yet we did esteem him stricken,*
> *smitten of God, and afflicted.*
> *But he was **wounded for our transgressions,***
> ***he was bruised for our iniquities**:*
> *the chastisement of our peace was upon him;*
> *and **with his stripes we are healed**.*
> *Isaiah 53:4-5 NKJ*

This is a prophetic Scripture given in the Old Testament concerning what the Messiah (Jesus) would accomplish though his death on the cross. It was written before the crucifixion happened, but interestingly, it was written in *past tense.* With God, there is no past, present, or future, all is the same to Him.

The Hebrew word for "healed" in verse five is *raphah.* The literal translation of this word is: *to mend by stitching, to cure, to cause to heal, repair, **thoroughly make whole.*** That means Jesus made a way for you to be made whole!

You can see how God covered *all* of our needs- all three parts of us-in these two verses. He took our grief and sorrows (emotions), He paid the price for our moral transgressions, or sins (spirit), and through His stripes He made a way for us to have physical healing as well (body)! All three at once were covered when He died for us on the cross! It just doesn't get any better than this!

I end where I began: God needs a healthy church. A sickly church is limited in the work it can do for His kingdom. Its people are not only unable to serve, but they are also a poor testimony and a poor representative of Him, and the world does not want what we are selling.

We know what God's purpose for His church is that we should *preach the kingdom of God, heal the sick, cast out demons, raise the dead, and make disciples*, and He has chosen to make *you* a part of it.

Do you know what role God has for you in this mission? Do you know *your* purpose? What has God designed *you* to do? If you don't know, ask Him; He will be faithful to show you.

You now have enough information to start the process of becoming the real you that God created you to be! My prayer for you, dear reader is that you will:

Test all things; hold fast what is good.
Abstain from every form of evil...
Now may the God of peace Himself
sanctify you completely;
and may your whole spirit, soul, and
body be preserved blameless
at the coming of our Lord Jesus Christ.
1 Thessalonians 5:21-23 NKJ

CONCLUSION

For those who wish to begin living the life God has planned for you, there is a sample prayer below in which you agree with God and ask Him to redeem *all* of your life, not just your spirit, but your soul, your mind, your emotions, *and* your body as well! His plan for your life can begin *now*, on this earth; you do not have to wait until you get to heaven! He wants a personal relationship with you.

Are you ready for a change? Do you want to be made whole? If so, you can pray something along these lines:

Dear Lord Jesus,

I trust that Your plan for my life is perfect. Please forgive me for wrong thinking and wrong living. I repent of my sins and ask You to cleanse my heart, my mind, and my body as You come and live in Me. I want to experience all that You created me to be and I desire to live for You from now on.

Please heal and restore my broken heart with the perfect love You have for me. I reject all fear, anxiety, anger and bitterness. Please heal my thoughts and emotions with Your perfect peace. I will never need to be depressed again or have a reason to give up hope because of what You have done on the cross for me!

I ask You to help me speak Your truth at all times and reject all conversation that does not build up or heal me, or other people around me. Purify my thoughts, my words, and my body so that I will be a healthy vessel that can do what You created me to do.

Help me to see myself each day just as You created me. Show me how to use all my gifts and talents for You.

Lastly, please help me to tell other people about what You have done for me so that they can know You and be made whole, too!

Thank You, Lord, for everything You are doing in me!
In the name of Jesus Christ I pray. Amen.

Congratulations! If you prayed this prayer and meant it from your heart, you are a new person; you now have the Holy Spirit living in you to guide you, direct you and give you power to do all the things you need to do! All you need to do is ask, and God will hear and answer whatever you need:

1 John 5:14-15 (NKJ) says: *Now this is the confidence that we have in Him, that if we ask anything according to His will, He hears us. And **if we know that He hears us, whatever we ask, we know that we have the petitions that we have asked of Him.***

You now have the Holy Spirit to regenerate every

part of your life; you have begun life as a new person: *Therefore, if anyone* is *in Christ, he is a **new creation**; **old things have passed away; behold, all things have become new.*** *2 Corinthians 5:17 NKJ*

To start your new life with Jesus, begin by reading the gospel of John and also the epistle of 1 John. The Scripture passages that have been discussed in this book will also help give you further insight into *all* of what Jesus has died to give you. Be encouraged, you are on your way to being made whole!

FURTHER READING

Walking in Divine Health, *Dr. Don Colbert*

Why Christians Get Sick, *Rev. George H. Malkmus*

God's Pathway to Healing the Immune System, *Reginald B. Cherry, Md.*

Bodily Healing and the Atonement, *Dr. T. J. McCrossan*

A More Excellent Way, *Dr. Henry Wright*

Bait of Satan, *John Bevere*

How to Handle Your Emotions, *June Hunt*

Deadly Emotions, *Dr. Don Colbert*

Commanding Your Morning, *Cindy Trimm*

Quick to Listen, Slow to Speak, *Robert E. Fisher*

Thirty Days to Taming Your Tongue, *Deborah Smith Pegues*

ENDNOTES

1. *thepuritanboard.com*

2. *sozotoday.com*

3. lifewithoutlimbs.org/about-nick/bio/

4. anxietycentre.com

5. http://peebles.wordpress.com/2007/11/29/let-the-weak-say-i-am-strong/